The Baking Soda Pancake

Written by:
L. Sarkozy

Cadmus Publishing
www.cadmuspublishing.com

Published by Cadmus Publishing
www.cadmuspublishing.com
Port Angeles, WA

ISBN: 978-1-63751-114-5
Library of Congress Control Number: 2021921611

CONTENTS

CHAPTER 1

THE

BAKING

SODA

PANCAKE

In August of 1975, I was dragging an industrial-sized garbage bag full of clothes down the streets of Nashville. At the end of every block, I would have to stop and wait for my big sister, little brother, and mother to catch up, as they too were dragging a trash bag. It was starting to rain, and as annoying as that was, it did help the bags slide down the sidewalk easier. We were carrying all of our little family's worldly possessions with us. This is where we ended up after a long chain of events had cascaded to put us on the streets.

Like any homeless family, it wasn't always like that. At one time, my father was a steelworker who worked at a foundry in Ohio, and my mother, a Mensa member, was enrolled in college part-time while taking care of us kids. My sister is a few years older, and my brother a few years younger, but we were all young then. One day, my dad began having intense headaches and would moan in agony at sunlight. Then he began having massive seizures. The foundry now saw him as a safety hazard, lest he have a seizure at work, and fired him.

I'm not sure of the actual mechanizations, but somehow my dad found a job all the way in Houston, Texas. Back in the '70s, cans of beer or soda had pull-top rings on them, and bottles were glass with little steel lids. My dad's job was to walk around the asphalt parking lot at the Astrodome and pick these items up, along with cigarette butts and any other litter. We could look out the window of our hotel room and see him, a tiny ant crawling back and forth on the massive sheet of asphalt, all day in the Texas heat. This didn't last long, however. After his first seizure, all alone out on the asphalt ocean, me, my brother, and sister went and did the job, and we kept doing it as my dad laid in the shade in agony.

It was finally discovered that dad had a massive brain tumor, which none of the surgeons would operate on. Dad was given the maximum doses of two anti-seizure medicines, but they had no effect. During this time, our mother had gotten us welfare and food stamps, so we got an apartment, which was good timing, because my dad's boss had seen us kids doing my dad's job, and although sympathetic, fired him.

At this time in my life, I had no idea that I would have bestowed upon me the wisdom of the Baking Soda Pancake, of which I may not be worthy. (Before jumping to conclusions about my mental health, we will get to the Baking Soda Pancake later, which is the star of this show.)

A world-famous surgeon from NYC decided he would happily dive into my father's skull and pop the tumor out, and incredibly flew to Houston on his own dime to operate. This was a result of my mom writing him letters and pleading with him. Although the surgeon warned that my father could die on the operating table, or become a vegetable, it was certain the tumor would kill him. The surgery lasted eighteen hours, and was declared a success.

By this time, our family was buried in debt. My dad still had, and would continue to have, massive seizures for the rest of his life, so my mom began the arduous and seemingly impossible process of trying to get disability for my father. Unfortunately, The Social Security Administration decided that a steelworker who only knows how to be a steelworker, but can't be one because he has two to three grand-mal seizures a day, was not disabled.

Being filled with optimism (because he was not dead), my dad decided we would make a fresh start. We moved out of our beloved Houston slum to Colorado Springs, Colorado. We kids were now old enough to attend school, and my mother began taking classes again. My father, who had given up on disability and steel working, began taking drafting classes in hopes of a new career. My older sister read the most books in the Muscular Dystrophy Read-a-thon that year, and was awarded with a plaque and a handshake from an astronaut. I joined the Boy Scouts, and had the privilege of camping out in the Rocky Mountains. My little brother joined Cub Scouts. It actually looked like the universe had given up on crushing us for a while, but alas, it hadn't.

My dad's tumor, which we thought was in a trash can in Texas, had not been fully removed; only a few cells were missed, and grew back with the intent of avenging their fallen comrades. After a few years of losing all we'd gained, my dad did not survive the second surgery. Now my young mother had mountains of debt, had to drop out again, and had to find a way to support three young children with no resources.

On a happier note, the Social Security Administration apparently does consider death a symptom of disability, and gave my mom a check consisting of money from when she first had applied. The checks were called survivor benefits, and from that point on my mom would receive a small monthly check to take care of her children. Not one to rest on her laurels however, my mom, who had been majoring in Early Childhood Development, had read somewhere that it was easy to open up a daycare center in New Orleans, so she decided we would move.

After paying off lots of debt, our now smaller family hit the road, and took a bus nonstop from Colorado to

Ohio where my mom had seven brothers and sisters. From there, we hopped back on a bus bound for New Orleans.

We had a layover in Nashville, Tennessee, when tragedy struck. Somehow my mom had lost our bus tickets, most of the cash we had, and the remainder of our survivor benefits check. This was before the invention of cell phones. My mom tried to call her brother for help, after dumping buckets of dimes for long-distance into a pay phone, but to no avail. Then, shining like the morning sun, she noticed a kiosk with a sign that read "Travelers Aid".

Without going into too much detail, well, make that any detail: you have a better chance of catching a ride hitchhiking with a bloody axe over your shoulder than you do getting any aid from "Travelers Aid".

My mom, never letting us see her sweat, told us we were leaving the bus station, though we, and she too, had no idea where we were going. Since our luggage consisted of all of our clothes stuffed into trash bags, we have made it back to the beginning of the story.

As we dragged our bags down the street, we got further and further away from the business district, and made it to an area with seedy motels. Our mom would tell us to stop, and she would run into the office of each motel. We could see her talking to the desk clerk in each one, gesticulating wildly and pointing at us. At about the fiftieth motel, my mom came out holding a key. She had given her wedding ring and her ID card as collateral, and had arranged for the next survivor benefits check to be sent to the motel, at which time the motel would take what was owed to them, and we would be on our way. Our next check was three long weeks away.

Before going any further, let's talk about eating. Here in America, we love to eat. We eat a lot. An American family of four probably throws out enough food in a year to feed a family of four in Bangladesh. It is hard for us to decide how much food we *should* eat. I will tell you, however, that a person, American or not, knows when they do not have enough food to eat. Our little family, due to the ingenuity of our mom, now had shelter secured, but food was another matter.

Most of the small amount of money that my mom had not lost had been gobbled-up by the bus station payphones. My mom began calling local churches. A local preacher pulled into the motel, and came up to our door with a small paper bag, and a lady holding a camera.

The man gave my mom the paper bag. It contained a jar of peanut butter, a can of corn, and a can of string beans. He then insisted my mom pose with him, bag in hand, so he could get a photo to show his congregation how enormous of a help he was to the downtrodden. My mom did, then cursed under her breath as she closed the door. The Good Lord was obviously busy tending to other matters, so we would have to find other ways to get food, and we did.

We had one of those old (new) Polaroid cameras, the kind where you push the big red button on the front, and, like a magic trick, the picture comes out of the front. My brother and I walked around trying to sell pictures to tourists for a dollar each. After we used up all of the film, we sold the camera too. It was in this way, and after employing many other hunter/gatherer techniques, that we kept squeaking by. We had made it to Survivor Benefits Eve, but it had not been easy, and we had not been eating nearly enough. Now, with only one night remaining before the check came, we were hungry, and had not been able to come up with any food for a few days. My little brother was laying on one of the two motel room beds, and repeatedly crying out, "I'm hungry mommy!"

For those of you who are fortunate enough to have never been truly hungry, count your blessings. Your stomach hurts, you have absolutely no energy, and you can taste nothing but toothpaste all day. You are minty-fresh, but miserable. This was the point we were at.

Seemingly oblivious to my crying brother, our mom got off the bed. She walked over to the mini-refrigerator and opened the door. The little light bulb in the refrigerator illuminated its only possession, a box of baking soda, which had probably been there since the Civil War. My mom removed it, closed the door, and turned to face my sister and I while saying "Heather, Lance, we are going to try to make some pancakes. Surely there are some ingredients we do not have, but it's worth a try. Will you give me a hand?"

My sister, being smarter than me, nodded solemnly that she would, so I took her lead and did too. My little brother immediately stopped crying, and leapt up, saying, "I want to help too!"

We mixed up the box of baking soda with water, debating the proper consistency. My mom put a big glob of it on my brother's nose, starting a tiny food fight; we were very careful not to waste too much. When we put a glob on the motel hotplate, it hissed angrily, and blew batter all over the place. Realizing this would never work, we spent the rest of the batter by slinging it at each other. When we were done, there was a colossal mess, but alas, not one pancake to be had.

My mom layed back down on the bed with my little brother. She stroked the hair from his eyes, telling him quietly to go to sleep, and to dream about all of the yummy food we would eat the next day. My brother, with a smile on his face and baking soda all over him, did.

My mom then covered him up, and with tear-rimmed eyes looked at my sister and I. She then whispered to us a thank you, and rolled over and went to sleep also.

This shocked me. The small chink in my mother's armor which she had just allowed me to see at once made me realize something; a mom is actually a person too, and this one was a scared young mother doing all she possibly could to take care of her kids, doing superhuman things with super human effort, as she had been doing all along, against massive odds. I at once silently vowed that I would try to behave better from that point on to help her, a promise that I would certainly break, but meant at the time.

It was not until I became an adult that I understood why a Mensa member tried to make a baking soda pancake. My mother died in 1998, and I never spoke to her about it. It was as if doing so would somehow tarnish the most ridiculous act of love I've ever seen, as if talking about it would change my belief that sometimes the belief in something, even if that belief does not change your situation, can at least change your outlook on it.

Besides the revelation that my mom was a human being, I also learned that if used properly, even a crusty old box of baking soda can become an inspiration. A horrible situation can yield an act of perfect love. This love, deep in your bones, can calm the hunger in your belly, and sometimes, but oh, so rarely, you may get something magical and special, if only you leave out a few ingredients.

CHAPTER 2

U.N.

AID

PACKAGES

New Orleans is one of the funnest places on earth, assuming one has money. If one has no money, one will find him/herself living in a big city slum, distinguishable from other city's slums in name only. Obviously, my little intrepid family found itself in a slum section. My mom, sister, brother, and I all lived in one room, and we shared a bathroom with other room-renters. That's because my mom had little money left over after paying for the new bus tickets and paying off the motel. Even so, this one-room home only lasted a few months, at which time we were able to move into an apartment, which was in a house that had been chopped up into four apartments. It had a living room, a kitchen, a bathroom, and a bedroom. It was in the same slum as the room was, but it was still the best we'd done since leaving Colorado, which already seemed like a thousand years ago.

Like after my dad's first operation, we began to regroup. My little brother was now old enough to go to school. My sister and I took a test, and we were both smart enough to enroll in a nationally recognized magnet school. When we got to New Orleans however, school only had one month left, which we did, and then it was summer.

Sometimes you can look back on something, and no matter how hard you try, you can't make sense of it. That is the case with my mom.

There was a man who lived in the apartment above us. His name was Don. He was, according to him, a Merchant Marine boat captain. He wore his white uniform everywhere, even to dive bars. The thing I can't figure out about my mom is how she ever fell for this guy, but fall she did. As soon as they were married, which was only a matter of two or three months, ol' Don immediately began to show his true colors.

Don was a violent alcoholic. He would drink white wine from the time he woke up to the time he went to sleep. He used to also hit my mom, who now stayed upstairs with him most of the time. For a boat captain, Don didn't work much. Luckily for Don, his new wife got a check every month. He finally got a job actually piloting a boat in the Persian Gulf, and quickly drove it into a sandbar. I'm not making this up.

Don obviously saw himself as our new Punisher. He'd hit us a few times, but not really bad, at first. Then he spanked me and my brother when he was drunk once using a belt, and from then on that was his preferred method, not spanking with the belt, but swinging it wildly.

I got a horrible job at a local grocery store. It entailed staying inside of a cooler all day long pushing new bottles of booze to the cooler's front. The store owner knew I was too young to legally work, and took advantage of that by only giving me a few bucks a day for my effort. One day, Don got drunk, found out where I was, and went to the store demanding the owner give him all the wages the owner owed me. The owner fired me.

It got to a point where my mom lived upstairs completely, and my brother, sister, and I lived downstairs. We would go upstairs to eat supper, and some days that's the only time we would see our mom. She was terrified of Don by this point, and had endured much physical and psychological abuse from him, so much so that she would pretty much back him in anything he did, lest he unleash on her.

One time they were arguing, and I went to our house's side yard and looked up. Don was smacking my mom around on the balcony, and she was screaming for help. I ran into our kitchen and grabbed a steak knife, then ran back to the yard. I screamed at him that I was sick of him and was going to kill him the first chance I got, brandishing the little knife. This boldness confused him for just enough time to let my mom escape. She ran out of the house and down the street, where she called the police. The police had been there many times, and never did anything. There were none of the domestic violence laws in place that exist today; all the police did was threaten me with jail because of my knife, and tell my mom to stay downstairs that night. When I woke up, she was already back upstairs.

One day, Don got drunk and he made some comment to my sister about what colors her nipples were. This comment, and the general state of things, caused my sister to run away; she was only about thirteen. Nothing seemed to infuriate Don more than my sister leaving, which tells me that it's probably a good thing she did. From that point on, he became a mad man.

My brother and I saw less and less of our mother, and food was becoming scarcer and scarcer. Sometimes my mom would drop small sacks of food from the upstairs into the side yard, like an U.N. aid package for refugees. As a result, I went and begged my ex-boss to take me back, promising him that Don would not know, and he accepted.

School had started again, so an average day consisted of me waking up, taking two different busses to school, walking around at lunch time, as I had no money for lunch, and then taking the busses home. I would walk straight from the bus stop to the store, spend seven to eight hours in the cooler, and try to steal food to eat while there. Then, I would take the measly money I made, and stop at Burger King, and buy as much of anything that I could. I would then take the food home and feed my little brother. This I did every day. I was eleven years old. Nobody ever asked me where I had been all day at that point.

One Saturday, I opened up the side-yard door, because I thought I heard somebody. The next thing I knew, I was on the floor seeing stars. Don had punched me as hard as he could on my forehead. He stood over me and said, "Hey, you little shit. Do you think I forgot about you pulling a knife on me? Your problem is you are too big for your britches. Let's see how tough you really are." He then punched me in my cheek so hard that it knocked me out. When I came to, he hit me about twenty times with his belt. Then he spit on me and left. Luckily, my little brother was off playing with a friend somewhere, or Don would have probably beaten him that badly too. My sister was still a runaway somewhere.

I remember laying on the kitchen floor, beaten, tired, and hungry, and wondering how much more of this I could take. I was a skinny, frail child, and Don was about 200 pounds, short, and stocky. I was truly contemplating murder; I could not runaway and leave my brother. How would he eat?

That night when I went to the store to work, the cashier, who was a sweet lady, stopped me as I tried to hurry by to go into the cooler. She pulled my hair out of my face and said, "Good God. What is wrong with that man? Do you want me to call an ambulance for you?" I replied that I was fine, and went to work.

A few days later, my brother told me that somehow Don had found out I was working at the store again, and to give me the message that he was going to beat my ass because of it. This was terrible news. I don't mean getting beaten again, I mean the fact that Don now knew about the store. This was the only way my brother and I had to survive. I made a decision, and I have never told anybody this before, but when I went to the store that night, I gave the sweet cashier a paper with my address on it, and told her that if she did not call the child abuse people, my brother, my mom, or I would certainly be killed before long. Two days later, a tall, slim, black man with a trench coat and wire-rimmed spectacles knocked on the door, flanked by two New Orleans policemen. Actually, he knocked on the door frame. The door had been kicked-in by Don so many times that it was just leaning against the wall. We had a large black and white t.v. with the screen kicked in, and a couch. The man identified himself as a detective, and he and the police walked in and looked at the wreckage of an apartment. My brother and I were sitting on the raggedy couch, which we had found in the trash.

After strolling around a bit, he stopped and said, "Hey son, look up at me." When I did, he saw my entire forehead was an angry purple, and my left eye was black. Then he told my brother and I to take off our shirts. I heard one of the cops sharply inhale when he saw my back. The detective then took pictures of us for evidence. He said, "Kids, you two will never have to live like this again," and then, "Follow me." Before we made it to his car, my mom and Don came running down from the upstairs apartment. Don said, "What the hell is this? Where are you taking my sons?" The detective said, "We are putting these children in state custody for abuse and neglect," at which point my mom screamed, "NO!" Don said, "You have no right to come in here and-" but before he could finish, one of the cops said, "Hey motherfucker, There's nothing I would like more than to fuck you up and bring you to jail. Get the fuck out of our way." Don, the big wife and child beater, said, "Yes sir," and did.

I so clearly remember driving in the back seat of the detective's car all the way to Belle Chase, Louisiana, where a foster home was ready to receive us. I was holding my little brother's hand the whole way, telling him everything would work out, and that this would surely give mom the courage she needed to escape Don. Inside, I was thrilled that for the first time in a long time I knew I would wake up the next day without worrying about getting beaten, or my brother starving. Not knowing where my sister was still worried me greatly, but maybe I could now find somebody to help find her. I was scared, optimistic, and absolutely full of anxiety all at the same time. Sadly, the hands of fate care little for how optimistic one may be.

Chapter 3

Becky

Under

The

Bridge

After getting settled in, our foster home was not that bad. My brother enrolled in the elementary school, and I was now in middle school. I made the middle school football team. I was perhaps the worst defensive end ever; I was lanky, skinny, and not athletic at all. Even so, it was really fun. My brother was not enjoying it much, though. He just did not like the foster mother's sons, and he really missed my mom.

I must say here that to anybody reading this, they would think my mother must be a horrible person. That is simply not so. My mother was the lady who turned baking soda into magic. The person my mother had become was a battered wife. Many times she tried to stop Don, and even absorbed our blows. Nonetheless, he had abused her psychologically also. She had lived in constant fear for both herself and us kids. This is something I did not realize at the time. When you combine the psychological and physical torture she endured, along with having no resources to escape with, and three kids in tow, she stayed with Don, not that he would have let her go anyway. Many years later, my mom would try to downplay the abuse Don inflicted after my sister left, as if doing so would somehow change it or erase it. I think she did this because, as brilliant as she was intellectually, she was still a human and a mother, and her mind would not allow her to admit how bad it had been for my brother and I. God knows how it was for my sister on the streets.

Every six months or so, there would be a hearing to decide if we should be returned back to the home. For a year, this was a non-issue, because our mom had to show that she had the ability to care for us, which was impossible with Don still in the picture.

Don began to make threatening phone calls to the foster mother, who was finally scared enough to tell the state that she could no longer keep us. Our social worker came and picked us up, and to my brother's and my shock, put us in different placements.

Here is how a placement works. If you are in state custody for abuse, you are put in a foster home. If you are in state custody because you are a child who committed a crime, you are placed in a group home. If you committed a serious crime, you go to a juvenile lockdown, and may transition out through a group home. Well, that's how it's supposed to work.

If you are a boy and at the age or past the age of puberty, foster homes do not want you. They want little kids that they may even adopt someday. Therefore, my brother was put in some 'temporary' placement somewhere, and I was lucky enough to get a foster home again, though it would be my last one.

This foster home was amazing. One single lady owned it, it was only blocks from the magnet school my sister and I had started, and I re-enrolled. The lady, however, after about six months, had to move because of work, and although she said that I could go with her, I decided to stay in New Orleans because of school. I was placed in a group home on Iberville Street, hated it and the junior criminals living there, and ran away.

My case manager was a lawyer. "I am *your* lawyer," he would always say. I went to a runaway shelter, but because I was only twelve at the time, they would not let me in. I called my lawyer, and told him on no uncertain terms that I would not go back to that group home. He called the runaway shelter, got some kind of age waiver, and they let me in.

The shelter was amazing to me. There were kids from all over the country who had run away for different reasons. One kid was fifteen, and had been to every state by way of riding trains. One kid had an arrest warrant where he was from; they would not extradite him, but they would arrest him if he returned home. It was also here that I met Becky.

Becky was a few years older than me, about the age of my sister, and she was absolutely lovely. She had raven-black hair and matching eyes, with alabaster skin. I knew she sensed how smitten I was with her, and as a result, used to let me follow her around. She had a boyfriend who was at least eighteen, and sometimes would vanish for days with him, and be morose and grumpy when she came back.

I tried to manage four different busses in order to get to school, but I was always late. I started to experiment with weed and booze, because everybody else at the shelter did. Then one day the shelter director told me I had to leave for two weeks; this was a policy that said if you stayed for a month then you had to leave for two weeks.

My lawyer came and picked me up, and brought me to one of the worst group homes there are. It was really a juvenile lock-up. I got in two fights while there, winning one and losing one. It took me seventeen days to devise an escape plan, which worked. Once I had made it to the ferry landing (the group home was on New Orleans' west bank) I called my lawyer and cursed him out. My lawyer talked me into meeting him, promising not to take me back. He picked me up and brought me to his house in Algiers.

My lawyer was openly gay, and I didn't care one way or the other about that. When we got to his house, he remarked that my hair was getting longer, and that I looked like a doper. He then told me that it was okay if I smoked weed. He said he was not testing me, as a matter of fact, he had some weed! He rolled up a joint, lit it, then passed it to me. It was homegrown garbage, but I didn't tell him I could get him much better. Then he gave me a beer, and encouraged me to drink it. Then he explained to me that he had only so much control over me, and I needed to stop running away. He told me I could stay the night if I wanted, smoking and drinking, then he'd try to find a 'nice' group home the next day.

I had said next to nothing until he said that. I snuffed out the joint and chugged the beer. Then, I stood up and said, "Check this out. I am going back to the shelter. If you ever put me in a place like that again, I'm going to have a talk with the judge about how you give dope and booze to young boys in your supposed care. If you think I'm joking, fuck with me and find out." He was completely silent. I walked to his door, opened it, and fired a parting shot, "Your weed is shit, dude."

I did indeed go back to the shelter. A few people there told me they knew my sister, and that she had been partying and I hoped I'd run into her. Becky was back also, but only had one night left before she had to leave for two weeks.

School was impossible to attend by this point. I spent my days stealing food from the French Market, practicing for when I knew I would need to. I panhandled, and didn't do that bad. People may not want to keep a teen boy, but they didn't mind giving one a few bucks, especially after I'd smear dirt on my face and muss my long and unruly hair. I learned from thieves, hobos, and most of all, other street kids how to survive on the street. When my two weeks rolled around again, I used every skill I'd learned.

At one point during my third two weeks, I ran into Becky. She asked me to go to a party with her, and she was going to tell the people there that I was her cousin. This party was in an area where I-10 meets Airline Highway. The apartment this party was at was practically under an overpass.

When we were let in, it was not much of a party; there were three guys and four girls, and they were all fucked-up out of their minds. They all seemed to know Becky, and she said hi, then gave me a beer. She told me, "Just chill out," so I sat down sipping my beer. Then one of the men pulled a tray out from under the couch with needles, rubber hoses, and a lot of heroin. I saw Becky's eyes light up in a way that scared me, and she rolled up her sleeve. To make a long story short, these people sat there and shot dope from eight o'clock until one in the morning. Becky said we were leaving (after all the dope was gone). Everybody else was passed out, and we left.

I had to keep steadying Becky as we walked. She said,

"Follow me," and we went into the maze of overpasses. When we got to a certain place, Becky walked over to a vent in the overpass wall, reached in, and pulled out a backpack. We walked a little further and sat down, cars on the highway buzzing over our heads. I kept looking around; this was a very dangerous place in a very dangerous neighborhood, though Becky seemed oblivious to it.

Becky opened her backpack and pulled out a rig. Then she reached into her bra and pulled out some dope, which she had obviously just stolen. She shot up and faded out. For the rest of the night, I stood watch as Becky shot up until all her dope was gone. The next morning, I left her at a bus stop, because she said she had somewhere to be.

I used my not less than formidable street skills to live on until my two weeks were up. Upon returning to the shelter, I weighed myself and was surprised to see I had actually gained a few pounds. Of course, the French Quarter was now getting dangerous for me. At least ten restaurant owners wanted to catch me for dine and dashing, and a few fruit stand owners in the French Market would yell and give chase every time they saw me. Still, I was never caught; I knew the streets better than the sidewalks did.

One day in the shelter, they called everybody together. The director told us that she had bad news. She said that some wino had found Becky under the bridge, overdosed and already cold; she'd probably been dead a few days when found.

I did not cry. I was too angry. I thought of my sister. I thought about how terribly unfair this world is, where a girl who looks like an angel destroys herself and dies among winos, broken glass, and used syringes. A world that lets me steal tomatoes to live, when I should be in school. A world in which my sister vanishes, like a wisp of wind, and it seems as if only I give a shit. A world in which help out of a situation puts you in one that is just as bad. I look back on my life, and I realize that it was at that point that my outlook on the world, people, and myself was set in stone.

I would end up in several different group homes and placements before I turned eighteen. At sixteen, I walked into Adult Education and took a GED test, which I passed. At seventeen, I enrolled in a local college, but cut class and looked at art pictures in the college library all day, and spent my bus money on weed. I did not care, at all.

I kept this attitude. Any person was either a mark, or a problem. I've been in literally more fights than I can count. I became a terrible person. Louisiana law will not allow a prisoner to profit off a crime if they are in prison. For this reason, I can only tell you that I am in prison and it is for a violent crime. The truth is, I should have been locked up years before I was. I was never equipped to succeed, only to survive, and sometimes being a survivor is a vicious endeavor.

I have written this tiny book from a prison cell. As I have, many old emotions have reared their ugly heads. This has been far from cathartic, but over the years I have learned to no longer rage. Yes, horrible things happened to me, but I have done horrible things also. My past is not an excuse for my actions.

I have been in prison for twenty-four years now, and it looks like I may finally be getting out soon. I have educated myself to a ridiculous level; I have several degrees and many federal licenses for communications. At age fifty-three, I believe that I am ready to make a go of it and live, not merely survive. People tell me how hard it may be, and I laugh inside, knowing that they have no idea how hard I've already had it.

Part of my optimism comes from the things that I have accomplished educationally. If a dog does something good and you pat him on his head, he will do the same thing again. People are different. If you pat a person on the head when they do something good, it is a fleeting thing. They will gain no self-esteem from the head patting. The only way that a person can gain self-esteem is by performing esteemable acts. My mother has been dead since 1998. Anytime I accomplish something, an esteemable act, I have nobody to pat me on the head anyway. I have greedily consumed my education with the same zeal as stealing a turnip from the French Market. One must take their experiences, good or bad, and attempt to apply them in a way that is good.

I have heard the cliche, "What doesn't kill you makes you stronger." This is absolutely not true. When a terrible thing happens to you, it chips a little part of you away. If enough bad things happen, you may be whittled down to almost nothing, but you can grow these parts back. They may be painful or misshapen, but given time, they will return. It may take a very long time, but even if it does, we should be grateful that we at least have the time to heal. Becky would have been.

CHAPTER 4

LIGHTS OUT

In spite of all I have written so far, like all kids, I did my best to have fun. When I was in my last group home and still going to Magnet School, I was very popular. The guys admired my almost psycho willingness to fight, and the girls saw me as some sort of Bohemian who did what he wanted, which, due to blackmailing my lawyer, I did.

On Friday and Saturday nights, my best friend, Roy, a girl named T and I used to drive around. T's mother owned an immaculate '75 Impala, pearl white and white leather interior. T was not really popular because she was a little overweight, whereas Roy and I were. We both grew our hair as long as any respectable hair band member, and we both had 3 earrings in our left ear. If we told T to, she would have driven off a cliff for us.

Instead of driving off cliffs, we had a pretty set-in-stone way we went about partying. Back then, the legal drinking age in New Orleans was eighteen. Nobody ever carded me past my fifteenth birthday, because I was tall and looked not less than a little crazy. We would go to a store and buy a fifth of Everclear and a one-dollar gallon jug of fruit punch. We would then drive around. T and Roy's families both had money, so that was never an issue.

Usually, we'd drive out of the city and hang around the lakefront at Lake Pontchartrain. Teens would park in a huge, circular parking lot we called 'The Point', smoke weed, drink, and mix. Heavy metal would be blasting out of the car stereos, and horns up the street would beep warnings to everybody when the police were approaching.

After going to The Point and finding hardly anybody there, we drove back to New Orleans. There was another hangout in Audubon Park, which we had named 'The Fly', though no one knew why. There is a football stadium there also, where high school teams would play. When we pulled in, it was packed. The parking lot was full of people partying, and there were clouds of weed smoke everywhere. Teams were playing football, and more teams were waiting to. The bleachers were packed with spectators.

Roy and I got out, immediately abandoning T, and talked to some people. Roy whispered to me that he had stolen a joint from his dad, but did not want too many lungs smoking it, so we looked for an unpopulated area. We saw the silhouette of a small building about a hundred feet away, and walked to it. It was perfect. We were about sixty yards from the stadium, in almost complete darkness. A family was playing volleyball fifty feet from us, but sensing we were up to no good, pointedly looked away from us.

Roy and I smoked, and we were really high. We started talking about all the dumb stuff teenage boys do, when Roy said, "No way! Look." I followed the finger he was pointing with; it ended on the little building's wall. We hadn't noticed before, but all of the circuit breakers to the whole park were on this wall. One said in huge red letters: MAIN, and it had a handle on it that looked like an airplane throttle.

Now, in my defense, any two American boys confronted with such a temptation could not refuse. I have seen that it is popular on the internet to tell your child to wait to eat candy that you put in front of them, and then leave the room to see what they do. Very few don't eat the candy. It's just not a fair test. Well, neither was Roy and I's situation a fair test.

Roy yelled loudly, "Three!" I yelled, "Two!" Roy yelled, "One!" and we both turned off every light in the park at the same time.

Hindsight is 20/20, but we may have gotten away with this were it not for the volleyball players, one of whom yelled, "Them white mother fuckers did it!"

Roy and I sprinted back to the parking lot, which was packed with mostly white kids. I clearly remember that almost everybody had their car radios turned to the local rock station, and "Bang Your Heads" from Quiet Riot was fittingly playing from at least ten different cars. We frantically looked for T, and saw her talking to some dudes. I ran over to her and told her, "We've got to leave NOW!" She looked at me in confusion, then went with me back to her car, which Roy was already in. I got in the back seat with Roy. As soon as T put her key in the ignition, four teams of football players came swarming into the parking lot, and began punching any white guy they saw. They smashed their helmets into any car. The fans were with them, and the lady fans were punching all of the girls. T turned to us and said, "You idiots did this, didn't you!" We responded by telling her to go. Go!

T backed up and began to weave through the chaos. We were almost free when a football helmet came flying through the air, bounced off the Impala's roof, and then continued to bounce off its hood. T hit the brakes. She exclaimed, "My fucking car! Those mother fuckers!" She then hit the gas and made a U-turn worthy of any Hollywood action movie, and drove *into* the crowd, intent on running over any football player she saw.

The Impala was met with massive assault, helmets being the weapon of choice. She pulled out of the fRoy, without killing anybody somehow, and began to turn again, but Roy and I grabbed the steering wheel and made her go straight, even though we were now in grass. After accelerating, we flew off of an embankment and landed on a jogging path. T stayed on this trail until we got to a small side street. We zoomed through traffic, the whole time looking back to see if we were being followed. Finally, T pulled over under an oak tree on an Uptown street. We got out to survey the damage.

The back and both left side windows were broken. There were dents all over the car, and each dent had a smear of color from the color of the helmets' impacts. Somehow a hamburger somebody had thrown was still on the car's roof. The little Impala hood ornament was gone, and most of the lights were broken. T began to cry, mumbling that she would be grounded until she turned eighty. Then she abruptly stopped crying, and her eyes got big. She said, "Did you guys know that one of those teams was Faucheux?"

We hadn't. Our school was too small to even have a football team, but about seven blocks up the street was Faucheux High School. Our school was very mixed; there were many whites, many blacks, and many Asians. Faucheux was all black. A white kid did not even dare to wait at a bus stop in front of this school. It was an inner city, low income and violent school. Sometimes kids from Faucheux would walk into our school in little gangs and rob people. This has nothing to do with racism, it is simply how it was.

T went home after we all three vowed that we would never admit that it was us. T made up a story about somebody vandalizing the car to tell her mom, who, as it turned out, was just thrilled that T had not been hurt.

Monday, as I pulled into school, I could see through the city bus window that there were little mobs of people walking around the school, all wearing Faucheux colors. As I tried to hurry into the building, some kid told me, "Hey Lance! Wow! I heard what you and Roy did at The Fly! There's a lot of people looking for you two!" I responded that I had no idea what they were talking about, and slithered into the school.

Roy and I managed to duck and dodge anybody we didn't recognize and after a few weeks, the hunters tired of the hunt, though me and Roy never admitted it had been us. T had the car fixed, and drove up to school a month later. The Impala was now glossy black. T explained she had begged her mom to change the color, lest it be recognized. T had also realized that neither Roy nor I were interested in anything to do with her other than her car, and never let us ride with her again. I guess she also thought that it's better to be unpopular and alive than popular and dead.

Roy ended up a meth addict, and I ended up in prison. T ended up a surgeon, bless her heart. She got a full academic scholarship, she'd told me one day when I just happened to run into her years later. She studied and studied, and made her dream come true, and I was amazed at all she had accomplished academically. Then, a strange, hazy look came over her eyes, and she said, "Hey Lance, remember that night at The Fly?"

This told me that in her new uber-successful adult life, she still looked back at that chaos as something special; maybe it was adrenaline, maybe fear, but it somehow stuck in her mind as exciting. Often, we see things in our past with rose-colored glasses, or see them in ways which they were not. All people are perpetually clawing through life, always looking for something profound, something meaningful. Sometimes we get lucky and find it, but usually we had it at some point, and just didn't realize it.

Whatever 'it' is, I believe that my sister found it. She has always loved animals, horses in particular. For years she has volunteered at an animal shelter, and is enrolled in college. I have so few pictures, but I have one of my sister when she is face to face nuzzling with a horse, her hair obscuring her features, but it is such a happy, peaceful picture. To this day I don't know what my sister went through when she had run away, and I will never ask her. I know what I had to do to survive, and I don't care to know how my sister did. I only know that she did, and that is plenty enough for me. Sometimes survival is only needed until you get something good, but to survive some things is the good thing itself. Becky did not survive, nor did she find what she was looking for in the euphoria of dope. I, too, looked within a joint or a bottle for answers, but there were only more questions. I have found, ironically, that the best way not to drown yourself in booze or smoke meth until your heart blows up is to just accept that life is not fair, it is not easy, and it can be downright terrible at times. The only way that life is fair is in that it is unfair to everybody. Like the healing I described earlier, being slow, so too must one put one foot in front of the other and march with no fear or trepidation to one's goals. They may make it, they may not. Bad things *will* happen, and when they do, one must march through them also. It is quite simple; if a person uses an excuse to never chase his dream, he will never achieve his dream. If a person overlooks, or pushes through obstacles, he *may* achieve his dream. 'Maybe' is all we're guaranteed, but it's better than nothing.

CHAPTER 5

MAYBE

AN

EGGPLANT

I possess excellent God Radar. Whenever I'm watching a movie or reading a book, my radar is constantly scanning for holy pings. God and I know each other pretty well too, although you won't hear Him talk about it.

The short time that my family lived in Colorado was amazing for a child, especially me. My favorite thing in the world at that time was dinosaurs. I read every book I could find on dinosaurs. I could, at age 9, identify virtually every known species that had been discovered, and tell you what era they had lived in. I had never wanted to be a policeman or an astronaut; I had decided that I was going to be a paleontologist.

Colorado Springs is in the foothills of the Rocky Mountains, which stand like a wall in the West, and the tabletop flatness of Kansas to the East. There was a fence that went around our apartment complex. Two boards were always gone, and if you went through them, you found yourself at the top of a steep hill. This hill was fabulous for sledding down in the Winter. In the Summer, I liked it more, because I could go hunting.

The hill itself was made of shale. At one time, around one hundred million years ago, this hill, now at 3500 feet of elevation, was underneath a great inland sea. The shale is layers of deposited sediment, and where there is this type of sediment, there are fossils.

Wanting to be a paleontologist, I spent countless hours chipping away this hill, looking for fossils. Mostly, and always, I would find tiny clam-like shells. I found so many that I threw them away. I found a tiny ammonite once, which was the prize of my collection. I had some fossilized leaves, a partial fish, and a large chunk of petrified wood that I had stolen from a National Park while in the Boy Scouts. My fantasy was to find a giant mosasaur or other such monster, but I had no luck.

After my mom told us we were moving to New Orleans, she told me I had to get rid of my "bag of rocks". Although I protested and tried to get her to see how great they were, she told me there was no way we were going to drag a hundred pounds of rock onto a bus. Luckily for me, my school had a field trip to Florissant Fossil Beds. I took my whole collection with me, and showed them to their head paleontologist. He kept the tiny ammonite, but told me the rest were either too common or too partial to be used. Even so, my tiny ammonite, I was informed, was an excellent baby specimen, and would be catalogued and put on display with their large ones. This thrilled me to no end, and I felt as if I were an honest-to-God paleontologist now.

It bears considering that billions of years ago, a star, having expended its fuel, blew up. All of the elements it had made, as a result of using all of the previously changed elements for fuel, blew into space. A tiny atom of iron ventured through the Universe, and finally got captured in the swirling mess of our infant solar system. Four and a half billion years later, a tiny sea creature grew, and happily took this iron atom to help build its shell. Obviously, the little creature died young, probably buried in an underwater mudslide, because the preservation was so pristine. It fossilized, and sat there, under rock, for another two hundred million years, until I found it. Two things are amazing about this story. The first is that it is true. The second is that it is true of *every* atom, not only in the fossil, but of a Toyota, and of you.

We are literally composed of, er, star crap. After we die, the atoms go on to do other things; some may end up in a giraffe, some in a mobile home. We don't know where they'll end up, or what they were before. For all I know, I could have an atom of iron in my ankle from the sword of a ninja, and a calcium atom that was once in a hippo's butt bone. How amazing is it that atoms come together to make us?

When I held that tiny ammonite, I knew none of these things. I only knew that what I held was incredibly ancient, and it blew my mind all that happened since this little creature had lived. Certainly, the creature saw itself as more than a random collection of atoms.

Becky had been much more than a random collection of atoms also, but unlike the ammonite, there is no proof that she ever existed. How many people have lived and died and nobody remembers? Certainly, more than are alive today. We cannot achieve immortality. Therefore, what is important is what effect we have on other people. As Becky had such a profound effect on me, she will at least remain real as long as I live, and if somebody reads this book, as long as they live, also. It is in how we live our lives that matters. Although it can be argued that an evil person, like Bin Laden, has achieved immortality by doing a horrific act, that's probably not how you want to be remembered.

Anyway, my knowledge of paleontology led me to thinking about lots of things. Sometimes I would stand on that hilltop, and imagine the mountains going back into the earth, and the sea covering up everything, with enormous and fantastic creatures swimming around. Then I would go further back, before the seas and land, to when the Earth was a molten sphere devoid of any hint that I would someday be here imagining it. I would ride my imagination back to the Big Bang, and then I would be at a loss. So much evidence supports these things. It would be impossible for me to deny the little fossilized creature in my hands, that I could touch and know it to be real. Who could believe in a God, or an Ark, or any other religion for that matter? No, that would be silly; I have proof of evolution in my very hand that is as solid as, uh, a rock.

The older I got, the more I studied science. I believe in science writ large, and believe that one day it may just save us from ourselves. The main appeal that science had for me is that it can't explain everything, nor does it claim to. There is a distinct possibility that there are areas that we as a species are just too dorky to ever comprehend, and I can accept that.

What really turned me off when it came to religion was when a person tried to 'save' me. I also hated that preacher who brought my mom peanut butter, and hated the Catholics for killing Galileo. I probably said, "I told you so!" every time a Catholic priest was caught in the child molestation scandal.

To me, God was not real; people who claimed he was were either stupid, misled, or trying to pull off a scam, and trying to indoctrinate me into any particular religion just pissed me off, because to me, that would indicate that I was seen as stupid enough to fall for it.

That is when my God Radar began to function. I could see when a movie was going to flip into full God-mode, and turn it off. I could tell anytime a person was about to ask me if I had been 'saved'. Beep! Beep! My radar was quite accurate.

As I've grown older, I still believe the things I did as a child. I believe, due to a mountain of supporting evidence, in how the Universe formed and we came to be. Nor have I ever joined any organized religion. I simply do not trust people to know things they cannot know, and then teach them to me.

However, I have changed my mind about God. I do not see God as a white-robed Santa look-alike. I do not know if it would be accurate to assume there is one God, as in how you can count one Buick Skylark, but studying science has led me to believe that there may be a force which causes things to happen. I don't mean winning the lottery or getting hit by a bread truck. I mean things like life itself. It is hard to look into the eyes of a cat and not feel as if he has some secret, a secret known only to cats. It is hard to imagine two weed heads out-running four football teams. As bad as I have been at times, I must ask, why am I still here? Are my atoms not bored of making me yet? Wouldn't making a Yeti be more fun?

In New Orleans, I was robbed at gunpoint three times. One of those times, the robber shot my friend in his face, but I escaped. One time, I was walking around a block, and there were police with guns drawn banging on a door. I knew the house, and told them, "That house is empty. An old man just died a month ago who used to live there." One cop told me, "We know. We have a reported burglary." Curious, I stopped directly in front of the door of the house to watch. The cops pounded on the door again. Immediately, somebody inside fired a fully automatic weapon through the door. There was no way I could not get hit, but somehow didn't. Another time a guy arguing with his wife shot holes in his apartment wall to scare her; all of the bullets whizzed past my head, but did not hit me.

Certainly, I do not believe that some God swerved the bullets away from me, but at the same time, there should be no way they missed. At least one bullet should have hit me on each of those occasions.

It's hard not to believe in something. The fact that you, dear reader, are reading this is absolutely astounding. If you were to pluck one atom at a time from yourself continually, at what point would You no longer exist? Is there a point where all of the things that make you who you are on a conscious level are erased by the physical world? Alzhiemer's disease indicates this is so. That means your mind and body are fantastically connected in such a way that defies comprehension. At some point, plucking one atom will erase you, as an entity, from the universe, and because you only knew exactly who you were, no one can miss you as much as you do, well, if you were still around to do so, but fear not! This does not mean that You no longer exist. Perhaps removing the atom simply stopped your body from being able to contain You any longer; we don't know.

What we can say is that the You part we are talking about can certainly be seen as your Spirit, and because there is no doubt we possess one while we are alive (or else you could not be doing the absolutely astounding and previously mentioned act of reading this), it would be a huge leap to assume we would not have, or be this same spirit when our bodies die. Either way, we can take comfort in knowing what we learned earlier; the last atom that we pluck from you that kills you will still merrily go on to make another amazing thing. . . like, maybe, an eggplant.

CHAPTER 6

PSYCHO

TURTLE

KILLER

When I was at the first foster home in Belle Chasse, I was allowed to hunt. The three boys of the foster mother were aged eighteen, fifteen, and nine, and all of them had hunted since they were wee tots. There was every size and gauge weapon that exists at that house. They used to go hunt deer in Alabama every few years, but in between, they would go into the local woods and hunt for squirrels and rabbits to stay sharp.

Even though I had never even held a gun before, my foster mom assumed I had, and let me go with the younger boys to hunt in the woods. I had a .410 gauge crack barrel shotgun. After watching the other people hunt, I finally took a shot at a squirrel who was way up in a tree. I missed terribly, and the squirrel looked down at me and chattered his disdain.

Eventually, I hit a few squirrels. The foster mom would skin them and save them, and then make squirrel stew. Yes, that's what I said. In all fairness, it was quite tasty, and you can taste the wildness of the squirrel. I realize most people would find this gross, but take my word for it; if you ever see squirrel stew offered at a food truck, eat yourself some.

Anyway, early one morning, I got the .410 and walked into the woods. It was still foggy, and I loved the woods. There would be enormous spider webs in between the trees with silver dollar sized yellow spiders sitting right in the middle of them. They do not bite people, but we'd still try to avoid them. We called them banana spiders, though I doubt that is their scientific name.

I was in a foul mood, because after wandering around for an hour, I had seen nothing to hunt, and had walked right into a banana spider's web, which had really freaked me out.

I stopped and sat down on a log. I saw movement out of the corner of my eye on the ground, and swung my shotgun to get a bead on it. At first, I couldn't see what had moved, then realized it was a turtle, who was about a foot in diameter. I walked closer to him and inspected him. I still had the shotgun pointed at him, loaded. I'd been told to not load the gun and carry it like that, but always did after I'd missed a rabbit because it had taken me too long to load the gun.

I wondered, in a completely academic way, what would happen if I put the shotgun on top of the turtle's shell, and fired it. I mean, I knew it would kill him of course, but would he explode? Would the blast bounce off of his shell? A .410 is a tiny gauge. Well, there was only one way to find out. I put the end of the barrel dead center on the turtle's back, looked away, and boom!

For anybody reading this who guessed the turtle blew up, you were wrong. The blast made a fist-sized hole all the way through the turtle. The turtle, who I had assumed would have been killed instantly, was not dead yet. The turtle extended his head, looked up at me, then went limp. I knew it was my imagination, but I could have sworn the turtle's expression was saying, "Really?" I knew a turtle is not capable of complex thoughts, has no facial features to convey emotions, and has no emotions, but I knew what I saw, man!

Anyway, the combination of the banana spider and the turtle ESP-ing me a message completely freaked me out. I dug a hole with my hands, and buried the turtle. I was sure to cover the grave with leaves to camouflage it, because if any of my foster brothers saw a turtle with a hole blown through it, they'd know it was me who did it.

Granted, shooting a turtle with a shotgun is not that wise, and quite messy to boot. I had to clean off the shotgun and my boots. After being sure that I had erased all evidence of the hapless turtle's demise, I left.

In spite of being asked to go hunting by my foster brothers several times, I kept declining. After a month, however, I gave in.

The nine-year-old and I were hunting together when he froze, smiled, and pointed up. I looked to where he was pointing, way up in an old oak tree, and there sat the biggest Louisiana Red Squirrel I've ever seen. He was just sitting on a limb and staring at us.

"Take 'em, Lance!" my foster brother whispered, "He sees me. I can't move."

I slowly raised the old .410, and put the red dot site on the squirrel's fuzzy little chest. From the short distance he was from me, he would end up with twenty lead pellets in him.

I slowly kicked off the safety, and put my finger on the

trigger.

I heard the turtle's ESP message, "Really?"

I began to slowly squeeze the trigger.

"Really?"

I could feel the trigger's tension ready to fire.

"Really?"

At the last millisecond, I aimed left of the squirrel by three feet and fired. BOOM! Leaves went everywhere and the squirrel shrieked, and vanished into the trees somewhere, as only squirrels can do.

My foster brother was livid, "How did you miss him? Nobody could have missed him! Did you see how big he was? How could you miss him? Aghh!"

Needless to say, it is impossible for me to hunt to this day. I never shot another squirrel, nor any other animal for that matter. Besides, it would be hard for me anyway, seeing as how I'm haunted by a telepathic turtle ghost. Now, don't get me wrong. I didn't turn all GreenPeace-y or anything. I love meat, and am a devout carnivore. I just don't see the point in killing a wild animal, whether he makes a tasty stew or not. After all, most convenience stores sell nachos that you can dump all the molten cheese your heart desires on to, and for a reasonable price. If there were wild nachos, I may consider hunting them.

It was entertaining for me to tote the shotgun around. It gave me a sense of power that I had never had before, which even at that young of an age, I realized was probably not a good thing. Of course, the foster brothers had been raised with these guns, and it was merely a way of life to them. A way of family life which was traditional. Does that make it right or wrong? I could argue that at one time, family life may have consisted of flipping over logs and dining on wood grubs together. The conversation probably sucked, but you got your protein fix. The difference is that hunting today is not to survive, but for 'fun'. I heard one hunter tell me he does it for the meat, and maybe he does, but by the time you buy a nice rifle, nice optics, trail cameras, ammunition, ridiculously expensive camo clothing, scent spray, and hunting licenses, you could have bought approximately seventeen cows. If you turned all seventeen cows into chili, you could dump that chili on 19,482 bowls of nachos; they come with all the melted cheese your heart desires, and for a reasonable price.

CHAPTER 7

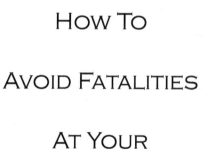

HOW TO

AVOID FATALITIES

AT YOUR

MARDI GRAS PARTY

When I was twenty-two, I was living in New Orleans' Tremé area. I was painting houses for a living, usually being paid cash under the table, and pretty much spending it as soon as I got it. One night I was at a bar in the Bywater area, nursing a pitcher of beer. I went to this bar a lot; I knew everybody there, and did work with many of its patrons. My friend, Tim, came in the door, looked around, saw me, and almost ran to my table saying, "Lance, check this out. I did some work at one of the t-shirt shops on the three-hundred block of Bourbon Street today. The lady that owns the place really likes me for some reason. She said that she had an apartment for rent. I asked her where it was. Guess where."

"I'm sure I don't know."

"It has two gigantic French windows that open up right on Bourbon Street! There is a balcony off the second floor, and you can look down on the balcony. Anyway, she wants $2,500 a month, but she says there would be no deposit for me, because I do so much work for her.".

"Okay, so why are you telling me all this?" I asked.

"I don't have $2,500."

"Forget it."

"No! Hear me out! I have $1,700. If you have $800, we can both move in and be roommates!"

"Look, Tim, I have a whole half of a shotgun house all to myself, and I pay $350 a month. Why would I want to pay $800, go through the hassle of moving, and end up in one tiny bedroom with a roommate?"

"Because, you idiot, Mardi Gras is in two weeks."

That hit me like a bolt of lightning. An apartment on Bourbon Street, during Mardi Gras! Imagine the epic party you could have!

"Exactly!"

"What?"

"You just said to imagine the epic party you could have!"

"Did I?"

"Yes!"

Well, to make a long story short, it was on. By the time Mardi Gras started, we were ready. We had two kegs of beer, a case of whiskey, a case of vodka, and a bunch of bottles of cheap wine. Tim had a small job rebuilding a bar room for a new owner, and instead of getting paid in cash, he got all of the open bottles of liquor the old bar had. We had twenty-five milk crates full of booze stacked up in our living room. We made up invitations, and gave them to all of our friends. The party was set for Mardi Gras day, at 7:00 PM, when Bourbon Street is jam-packed and everybody is at his or her craziest.

Before going any farther, I must tell any pretty young lady that comes to New Orleans that there is an old Mardi Gras tradition. If you go to a parade, they throw cheap plastic beads at you by the thousands. Every once in a while, they pull out a really nice set; they are big and gaudy, and look like 1920s costume jewelry. The masked people who throw the beads will point at a pretty girl, and if she flashes her hooters at them, they throw her the beads. This knowledge of beads and hooters is important further on in the story, along with the knowledge that Tim and I had easily 500 of these beads.

Tim and I were sitting in our Bourbon Street overwatch, waiting for our guests to arrive, looking down at the milling throng of drunken humanity. By 6:45, nobody had shown up.

"Lance, we gotta do something! Nobody's here!"

He was correct. As my eyes first looked at our mountain of booze, they wandered to the Hefty bag in the corner.

"Tim, I've got it!" I exclaimed. I grabbed the Hefty bag, which was full of five years of collecting the best beads, and grabbed the hundred or so invitations we had left over. I affixed an invitation to a bead, and said, "Watch this!"

Tim and I went to the window, and began to dangle a handful of the fancy beads. Suddenly, five or six different girls flashed us, and reached up for their beads. Tim and I shared a diabolical smile of understanding. We picked one girl, and threw her the invitation-laced bead. She read the invitation, and she yelled, "How do I get up there?"

Tim yelled back he would buzz her through the security gate. Thirty seconds later, we had three nice-looking, half-drunk girls in our apartment, looking in awe at our mountain of booze. They asked why, if this were a party, how come it was only me and Tim there? We told them, and the next thing we knew, we now had five bead fishermen, er, fisherwoman.

Within a half-hour, we had our party. There were at least a hundred people in our humble abode. Our booze mountain was eroding away quickly. Our two giant windows were jam-packed, and we had to keep making people step back, lest they fall to their death. Fatalities always wreck a good party. Oh, the humanity! One guy was walking around with a camera filming everybody. Several women had no shirts on. One guy, with an Idaho State University shirt on was passed out by the beer kegs with one shoe missing. Concerned parties drug him into the stairwell, where there were already three others passed out. That's when we heard one of our guests yelled, "Oh yeah! Well, fuck you too!" and then the unmistakable sound of a breaking bottle. I ran (er, figure of speech) to the window, pushed people out of the way, and saw that the yelling guy had thrown a bottle of vodka at our downstairs neighbors, who were on their balcony, looking up at our windows in terror. One of the neighbors said something about being a gun owner and calling the police at the same time. As is commonly known in the profession of debauchery, the only thing worse than a fatality at a party is a cop.

I grabbed the guy and pushed him, and told him to get out. He said something stupid, and I punched him. To this day, I have no idea how that started every guy in the place fighting each other. All the women panicked and ran for the apartment's little door as the guys kept fighting. I became enraged that this guy had just ruined Tim's and my party, and started fighting like a crazy person. Tim was a pretty big boy, and did his part. In a matter of minutes, every guest was gone, well, except for the four passed-out guys, but we'd forgotten them. Tim and I then walked down the stairs, chasing any stragglers out, until finally everybody was back on Bourbon Street. Tim and I went back upstairs.

I have no idea how the cops got past our security gate, but three of them came running into our apartment, guns drawn, and told us to get on the floor. Our terrified downstairs neighbors were cowering behind them.

After the cops were satisfied there was nobody there with an Uzi, they let us up. We told the cops some guys we didn't know threw the bottle, and our neighbor said it was not us, whom he knew. We also told the cops that they had tried to beat us up (as we were pretty banged up), and wrecked our place (as it was pretty wrecked), but we were sure they left.

I have no idea who that University of Idaho guy was, but bless his heart, he had really bad timing when it comes to sobering up. Apparently, one of the four passed out guys had come to, and having no idea where he was, woke up the others to find out. All four staggered into the apartment at the same time.

"That's them!" cried the neighbor. Tim and I exchanged a glance.

The cops leapt on them, both cuffing them and clobbering them at the same time. The Idaho guy, still being very drunk, yelled out, "Where is my shoe? Where is my shoe?" The cops hauled them away, and told me I had to go file charges at their station. I told the cops I wouldn't, and the neighbor, now that he knew he would not be killed the rest of the night, to my surprise, didn't want to press charges either.

We were not surprised to find out we were evicted the

next day, but didn't care anyway; I had never moved my stuff from the $350 a month place. I let Tim stay with me until he got another apartment. The $2,500 a month Bourbon Street apartment had been trashed, we had guns pointed at us, drunk people almost fell to their deaths, there was an enormous fight, innocent people almost faced felony charges, two escaping girls had been trampled, and all of our booze was gone. All in all, a pretty successful Mardi Gras party. Since we only got the apartment to have one party, we got Tim's clothes, and left it trashed, except for one size 11 deck shoe Tim found. He still has that shoe to this day. A bizarre Only In New Orleans type of trophy awarded for Best Party of the Season.

You must understand; this is not just a shoe from our party casualty, this is a shoe from a *tourist*. New Orleans has a love/hate relationship with tourists. Simply put, they love the money tourists bring in, but hate them as, well, people, probably because so many people have to rely on their money.

Take Chief, for example. He was a good friend of mine, a full-blooded Cherokee. Everybody (quite unimaginatively) called him Chief. Anytime we'd walk down the street, and a tourist would ask for directions, Chief would give him directions which would lead him straight into the Iberville Housing Project, where he was sure to get robbed. When I asked Chief why he did this, all he'd say is, "Fucking tourists," and that was a sufficient answer for a New Orleanian.

New Orleans is two cities, the one the tourists see, and the one that people live in. It can be very dangerous at times, like all big cities, but if you read a tourist guide, all you see are the lovely parts; they would never show you the bad, of course. That would be like an advertisement for vacation in Rio, and instead of perfectly tanned models frolicking on the beach, they showed the slums that the greater number of their population lives in. Rio is just like us.

We try so hard to be sparkly and attractive. We try so hard to impress. We try so hard to be *seen* as the tan model, even if we are, or feel like we are, the slums. This is probably a good thing, or else we would all act like we felt, like, uh, Tim and I did. What makes people great, and this includes you, dear reader, is not that we all aren't at least a little slummy inside, it is that we recognize it and try to be better.

I think it was Aristotle who said that we are a sum of our experiences. Everything you have ever done, learned, did do, didn't do, or thought about makes you who you are, and that's pretty darned special. There will never be another you, and luckily for turtles and University of Idaho students, another me either. Because I have learned from all of my mistakes, mathematically, I have to be a genius at least. So don't fear the future. You can take it from me, and I'm a college graduate. I'm also an abused child, a foster kid, a street urchin, an epic party thrower, a prisoner, and a slayer of Impalas, squirrels, rabbits, turtles, and University of Idaho students. If you can't trust me, who can you trust? What was that? Oh, sure I do! Just go to the corner, cross St. Claude Avenue, and keep walking straight. By golly, you'll be there before you know it!

Chapter 8

The Saga

Of

Zanax

The Rottweiler

When I was around twenty-five, I had been doing a lot of renovation work, and now had my own customers, and two contractors I could work for anytime I wanted to. I had a truck, and an apartment on North Peters Street in the 9th Ward, which was right across the street from the Mississippi River's levee.

One day, I came home and I heard a yelping sound coming from under the house. I looked to see what it was, and saw a tiny, black shape. I had a 9 mm. handgun, and thought about getting it, because I thought it was a huge river rat. Before I could, out walked the most adorable little puppy I'd ever seen, and he began yelping at me. I picked him up, and looked around, seeing nobody, or any other puppies. I put him in my house and gave him some water, and then got a flashlight.

I looked under the house with the flashlight, expecting to see a mess of puppies and a mommy dog, but there was nothing. I had no idea where this pup had come from, but I already knew I was going to keep him. It was love at first sight.

Which I did. I took him to a friend of mine who was a vet, and he got his shots for free. The vet said the puppy was certainly a full-blooded Rottweiler, and would grow much bigger. My friend was also a pill junky, and, even though he knew all I did as far as drugs went was to smoke some weed sometimes, he asked me if I knew where he could get some Zanax. I had no idea, but for some reason, I really liked that word, so I named the puppy Zanax.

Everybody that I know thought that naming the Rott Zanax was hilarious for some reason. One friend told me, "What else did you do? Name your cat 'meth'?" I, however, and Zanax, loved his name, so there.

Zanax was amazingly smart. Whenever I tried to teach him something, he would lock his eyes on whatever I was doing in an effort to focus. Zanax, the cute puppy, also grew. Within a year, he was a giant, but he was still sweet and goofy, and never once even growled at people.

I took Zanax almost anywhere I went. If I could, I'd take him to a job site, tell him to stay somewhere, and he would not move. If I went out partying, I would take him into a bar with me, and all the people would love to pet him, especially when they realized what a gentle giant he was. At home, he would sleep on the foot of my bed, and lick my face to wake me up each morning.

I had never loved any animal more than I loved Zanax. [Editor's note: Do not take the above sentence out of context.] He was my partner. He was always in a good mood, and he always made me smile. Unfortunately, Zanax was also too smart for his own good.

I had a screen door on the front of the apartment. I just left the door itself open all the time, because the screen door was actually a screened, steel burglar door. I had taught Zanax how to open this door so he could go use the doggy bathroom anytime he wanted to; he never stRoyed from the yard, which he no doubt considered his.

One day, I had to go do a job further in the city, and after I gathered up the tools I needed, I went to my truck, only to see that all the air in one tire had escaped the night before. I knew the tire had a leak, but didn't have time to fix it. I decided I would have to walk around fifteen blocks to a main street, named St. Claude Avenue, and then ride the bus from there. I told Zanax to go inside, then I began my trek, carrying a pile of tools with me.

I made it to the bus stop, and sat down on the bench. Instantly I could see a big, black mass running down the street. It was Zanax, who had obviously let himself out and then decided to run after me.

I yelled at the top of my lungs, "Zanax! Stay!" but knew he could not hear me over all the traffic on this four-lane street. Zanax, tongue flopping back and forth, eyes locked on me, never even saw the bus that was flying down the street. I heard the impact, screamed, and dropped my tools and ran across the traffic. Zanax was nowhere to be seen. Some guy that was sitting on a stoop said, "That dog ran off that way, he looked bad!" The man had pointed back towards my apartment. I ran fifteen city blocks to my apartment, leaving my tools there on St. Claude. I ran into the apartment: no Zanax. I looked under the house: no Zanax. I then began calling him and peering under every house all fifteen blocks back to St. Claude: no Zanax. I expanded my search area to side streets and parallel streets over the next few days, but never found him.

Finally, I gave up. I knew he had hid somewhere and died like many wounded animals do. I wondered if he thought about me, who had been his best friend his whole life. I hoped so.

I never got another dog. I had loved that dog more than, by far, most people I know. He never argued with me, he never drank my last beer, he never turned me down for sex. Okay! I'm just kidding of course! Seriously, he was one hell of a dog, and I miss him to this day. I like to think that maybe I'd made his life a little better, too.

For those readers who were expecting a happy ending, I'm sorry to disappoint you, but, once again, life is not fair. When you lose something you love, it leaves a hole in your heart. When you lose someone that you love, it is much worse. Just like I said in chapter three, when a bad thing happens to you, it chips off a little part of you, but nothing takes as big a chunk out of you as losing somebody you love. This wound also takes the longest to heal, although at times in your life the wound's pain might come back full-force.

On September the 25th, 2015, my little brother, Shane, left this world. I may have been closer to him than anybody else in my life. Of course, I love my sister just as much; it's just that Shane and I had survived after my sister smartly ran away, and since then I've always felt some sort of almost parental love for him. I messed up a lot, but my brother still stood by my side, even though I didn't deserve it. The pain of his death I can not in any meaningful way describe, but it has eased. If you are going through such a loss, know that it *will* ease, but never go away. As well it shouldn't. After all, the people we love help to make us who we are. We share our accomplishments with them, and cry over our defeats. When they go, you are more alone. If you really think about it, you may have five, or ten tops, people in your life that if they died, you would be crushed. We never expect it to happen, but it most certainly will.

So, stop wasting your precious time reading this stupid book. Instead, tell the ones you love that you love them, and stop arguing. Life is too short. Make it a good one.

CHAPTER 9

BACK

TO

NACHOS

Dear reader, if you are still reading this, then you either did not obey my last paragraph, or you live alone and nobody loves you. Either way, welcome back.

I decided to write about the events that I've covered because I learned some sort of lesson in all of them, except for Tim's and my party. I put the party in because I want to make clear that this party was not an exception to an ordinary life-style, it *was* my life-style. I was always trying to out-work, out-fight, out-party, out-xxx anybody else. I was not doing this for what a normal person would call fun. I did things like this because I was so messed-up inside that it was the only way I felt alive. When I said that my attitude changed after Becky O.D.'d, I meant it. My only philosophies were Fuck the World, and It's All About Me.

In my defense, I had to have that attitude in order to survive as a child. I never grew up inside. Age is a mandatory thing, whereas maturing is optional.

I left a lot of wreckage in my wake, some of which can

never be mended. As I've grown older, I've tried to mend some things, with varying degrees of success.

I used to say anything that popped into my head. Can you imagine a world in which people actually said what they thought, instead of what they thought they should say? Consider the following conversation:

"Hello Jane! This is my friend, Jerry, I told you about!"

"Oh, hi Jerry! I've heard so much about you!"

"Oh my! All good I hope!"

"Absolutely! Fred told me you are a great employee, and you're going places."

"Thank you, Jane. I hope I live up to his expectations."

Now consider the same conversation if people actually said what they thought:

"Hello Jane! This is that guy, Jerry, Fred hired to spy on us."

"Oh, hi Jerry. Have you always been this short?"

"What do you care? I've heard about you, slut."

"I don't care, you dwarven scumbag. I hope Fred fires your ratting ass."

"Thanks a lot. I can always become your pimp."

Now, perhaps I exaggerated a wee bit, but not much. All we do is judge each other, and usually harshly, and with a negative connotation. For most of my life, I let it fly. Now I say little, but listen much. You learn much more with a closed mouth.

I always had great potential. At my last group home, my I.Q. was tested at *almost* genius, whatever that means. Does that mean I can *almost* solve a Rubik's Cube? I don't know.

What I do know is that I used my brains solely to manipulate those around me for most of my life. Now, I have amassed an enormous education, too lengthy to even begin sharing. Just know this: potential is worthless unless it is applied to something (preferably something positive).

I think we all want to be better people, and by this I mean everybody, not just in some small area of our life, but in a much more macroscopic way. Our egos push us to want to be seen as good, and our psyches push us to try to become what we are acting like we are. Although I previously stated that life is an unfair endeavor, it is just as true that most people are good. Sure, our old genes may make us competitive for forage and mates, but inside, we are all closely, terrifyingly closely, similar to each other. We all laugh, and we all cry. It is these two qualities which make us human, even if some of us drive a Gremlin. (Yes, they are too human!)

I end this impersonation of a book with a cautionary note. If you see some idiot, say, calling Jerry a "dwarven scumbag", have pity on that person. I have shown myself that some of the worst people (like I was) can also be people who are the most torn-up inside. Have a little mercy on them, and a little mercy on yourself. I know from experience that nothing took the wind out of my evil self's sails more than a person being nice to me. You almost can't help but to be nice back, or you feel like a dick. Being nice is easy. All you have to do is bring the bad guy to your local convenience store and buy him a bowl of nachos; you can put all the melted cheese on them you like, and at a reasonable price.

ABOUT THE AUTHOR

L. Sarkozy holds the General Radiotelephone Operator License with Ship Radar Endorsement, the highest FCC commercial license. He holds Chief Examiner status for the National Radio Examiners, and has C-Tech certifications in copper and fiber optics. He was inducted as a member of the National Society of Collegiate Scholars, and is a graduate of and currently enrolled at Ashland University. He loves nachos, too.